The Urban Explosion in Latin America

A Continent in Process of Modernization

Principal Cities in Latin America